COME

Peasant, King

An Advent Devotional

f

THE FOUNDRY
PUBLISHING®

TABLE of Contents

Every year Christians prepare for the birth of Christ. We remember how Jesus was born to Mary and Joseph. We reflect on the beauty of the incarnation—God becoming human and dwelling among us. We often celebrate the greatest gift by giving gifts to one another. We do this every year. Advent helps us prepare for the birth of Christ again and again.

Advent isn't just preparation to remember a past moment. It is also a season when we look forward in hope to the second coming of Christ. The incarnation is a sign and symbol of the willingness of God, the Creator of the universe, to enter into our lives. This willingness wasn't just a one-time event. It changes everything for those of us who follow Jesus. Although this is a core focus of the Advent season, perhaps we ought to reflect on the second coming of Christ every day of our lives— not in trying to predict Christ's return or attempting to read the "signs of the times" or using anything and everything as an excuse that confirms the end is near. Instead, we should seek to order our lives in preparation for the new heaven and the new earth toward which Scripture points us.

 action

God's willingness to come and to come again is an invitation to us to live as if God is here now. God-with-us isn't a past experience or merely a future hope—it is a current reality. But to live this way requires that we respond to what God has already done, is doing, and will do; and it also requires a willingness to give ourselves fully to God.

This Advent season, as we remember the great gift of the incarnation and look forward to the return of our Lord and Savior and the renewal of all things, may we prepare by living faithfully and recognizing that all are invited to discipleship. May we participate in the redemptive work of God through the incarnation and in our anticipation of the culmination of God's work in the world.

So come, peasant, king, and everyone—come and follow the one who was, who is, and who is to come. God is with us. Will the shape of our lives reflect this truth?

FIRST SUNDAY OF ADVENT

November 28, 2021

SCRIPTURE READING

PSALM 25:1–10

I offer my life to you, Lord.

Make your ways known to me, Lord; teach me your paths. Lead me in your truth—teach it to me—because you are the God who saves me. I put my hope in you all day long. Lord, remember your compassion and faithful love—they are forever!

God guides the weak to justice, teaching them his way. All the Lord's paths are loving and faithful for those who keep his covenant and laws.

—PSALM 25:1, 4–6, 9–10

Sometimes the world seems really dark and impossibly broken. Sometimes our families seem beyond hope and beyond repair. There are times when our churches are divided and bitter instead of united in love of God and neighbor. Sometimes our work feels meaningless and unproductive. The psalmist feels it too. There is shame, there are enemies, there is treachery, there is sin, there is injustice in Psalm 25. We can relate. But what do we do when all around feels like despair?

At Advent, we light a candle. The light of the single flame is a reminder to us of the in-breaking hope that flickers in the darkness of our world.

Of course, this isn't the only light that shines. There is hope all around us and within us as we remember again the incarnation of Christ, God with us, Emmanuel! There is hope all around us and within us as we anticipate the second coming of our Lord; the new heaven and the new earth; all things made new! There is great hope.

The psalmist reminds us that the difficulties of life bring hope too: God is trustworthy! God is our teacher! God's path will become our path! God is compassionate and forgiving! God brings justice to the weak! God is loving and faithful! There is great hope.

But the hope of Advent isn't just for those of us already worshiping God and gathering in communities of faith. It is meant to be a light that spreads and grows, transforming the shadowy corners of our world with life and light. If we simply light a candle in our sanctuaries and walk out the door unchanged, how will the world know of the Christ who is with us and the Christ who is coming again? Maybe we can find the answer in these seven familiar words: "I offer my life to you, Lord." This is where the psalmist begins, and it is where we need to begin this Advent season. In the face of the darkness, brokenness, divisiveness, suspicion, fear, sin, broken systems—in the face of all of that and more, may we say with the psalmist, "I offer my life to you, Lord."

These are the kinds of words many of us have prayed at altars or bedsides. Isn't this what you do when you ask Jesus into your heart? Isn't this what it means to be saved? Aren't these seven words the same ones that invite the Holy Spirit to sanctify us, to fill us with love, to shape us into the image of Christ? We might think they are common words because we have used them and heard them and believe them. May we be reminded that these are *not* common words—instead, they are words of radical discipleship. They are the revolutionary work of the kingdom of God. These words change everything.

You don't have to look far in the pages of Scripture to find that, when a person commits their life to God, everything changes. They are called to move. They are invited to speak. They are compelled to stand up against injustice. They birth babies who were unexpected but desperately prayed for. They are mocked and scorned because of their obedience. Some are even killed for offering their lives to God. Everything changes when we live into these seven words.

Not just saying these words but really *meaning* them implies we will trust in God and no one else. We won't trust in our abilities or our intellect—although those can be used by God. We won't rely on our finances or our possessions—because those are God's anyway. We won't lean on our favorite political agenda or party to save us—because we know those systems are not kingdom-of-God systems. We will trust in God. And, like the flickering of a lone candle in a dark room, our trust may feel small and weak, but the more we seek God's grace and offer our lives to him, the more our trust will grow. As it does, we will experience the hope that only comes from the God who has come, is with us, and is coming again.

During World War II, a dark time filled with despair, Maria Skobtsova became a nun. She longed to help refugees and the poor as she sought to follow Christ. She was instrumental in saving the lives of many Jews who would have been sent to the gas chambers. Later arrested and sent to the Ravensbrück concentration camp, Mother Maria was ultimately executed by the Nazis. Before her arrest, she penned these words: "I am your message, Lord. Throw me like a blazing torch into the night, that all may see and understand what it is to be a disciple."

May our lives be a flickering candle or a blazing torch in the darkness of our world as we hope expectantly and shine forth the light of Christ for all to see. This Advent season, let us say and truly mean: "I offer my life to you, Lord."

FOR REFLECTION OR DISCUSSION

1. In your life, where do you feel hopeless? What seems insurmountable right now?

_____

_____

_____

_____

_____

_____

2. Where can you see a flicker of hope, however small, in the world around you?

_____

_____

_____

_____

_____

_____

3. What would hold you back from offering your life, fully, to the Lord?

_____

_____

_____

_____

_____

_____

Monday, November 29, 2021

SCRIPTURE READING

JOHN 9:1-7

As Jesus walked along, he saw a man who was blind from birth. Jesus's disciples asked, "Rabbi, who sinned so that he was born blind, this man or his parents?"

Jesus answered, "Neither he nor his parents. This happened so that God's mighty works might be displayed in him. While it's daytime, we must do the works of him who sent me. Night is coming when no one can work. While I am in the world, I am the light of the world." After he said this, he spit on the ground, made mud with the saliva, and smeared the mud on the man's eyes. Jesus said to him, "Go, wash in the pool of Siloam" (this word means sent). So the man went away and washed. When he returned, he could see.
—JOHN 9:1-7

Have you ever experienced complete darkness, where your eyes are open but you can't see anything? You know where you are, but everything feels different. Your ears suddenly hear sounds you normally miss— your pounding heart, the quickness of your own breath.

For those of us with the ability to see, complete darkness can quickly become overwhelming. For some, on the other hand, darkness is a way of life. In our world, being blind has both disadvantages and advantages.

There is danger and lack of opportunity, and there are challenges in the path of one whose vision is impaired. But there are also some advantages for someone who lives blind in a seeing world. Those of us who rely on our sight often find ourselves overwhelmed by our other senses that are awakened and heightened in the darkness, but those who live without sight learn to perceive the world around them in ways that those who have sight often miss. Vision isn't everything.

So why would Jesus heal the man born blind? If vision isn't everything, why not leave him be and teach the disciples that there is more to life than seeing? Jesus needed to address the reality that plagued the world around him: to be blind, or not able-bodied in some other way, was understood to be a sign of and punishment for sin. Jesus made clear this is not so. And, before we think we have matured beyond this thinking in our age, we must recognize the ways we still prefer the able-bodied in our churches, workplaces, schools, and communities. We may not attribute the differences to sin, but contemporary society certainly struggles to honor, dignify, provide for, and celebrate those differences in our lives. We lack vision.

Jesus—in the midst of reshaping the disciples' understanding of sin, affliction, disability, and God's goodness—says these words: "While I am in the world, I am the light of the world." In our passage today there is a man who has no physical vision, and there are disciples who have the wrong spiritual vision. Jesus, the Light of the world, is here to bring healing for both.

In Jesus's day being "whole" in the eyes of society was crucial. To be blind or disabled in any way came at great cost to one's place in the community. This isn't too different from our world today, which often values the able-bodied above all. We need the healing work of God to open our spiritually blind eyes. We need to recognize that Jesus is the Light of the world. We need our blindness to be made into holy sight for the glory of God. Our vision isn't healed for our sake alone—it restores the community that only comes as we allow Christ to be the Light of the world.

Blindness made it impossible for the man to be part of the community of faith because of their view of sin—but Christ brought healing. Spiritual blindness kept the disciples from seeing the true nature of God's community—but Christ brought healing. May the eyes of our hearts be opened and God's community formed in us as we together follow the Light of the world.

FOR REFLECTION OR DISCUSSION

1. Are there people who don't fit in for one reason or another at your church? How can you work to help bring healing to the community you are part of?

_____

_____

_____

_____

_____

_____

_____

2. It is so hopeful that Jesus is the Light of the world. What are some places in your life, your community, that need that hope? How can you shine Jesus's light in those places?

_____

_____

_____

_____

_____

_____

_____

_____

_____

SCRIPTURE READING

MATTHEW 5:13-16

You are the salt of the earth. But if salt loses its saltiness, how will it become salty again? It's good for nothing except to be thrown away and trampled under people's feet. You are the light of the world. A city on top of a hill can't be hidden. Neither do people light a lamp and put it under a basket. Instead, they put it on top of a lampstand, and it shines on all who are in the house. In the same way, let your light shine before people, so they can see the good things you do and praise your Father who is in heaven.

—MATTHEW 5:13-16

When you bite into something that isn't well seasoned, you almost know instantly if there is too much salt or not enough. Similarly, I'm sure we all have experienced groping in the darkness for something we cannot see without the light. Salt and light are ordinary parts of our everyday lives. Too much or too little of either, and we become painfully aware of their inherent value at the right quantities or levels.

What does it mean for the followers of Jesus that he calls us salt and light? Perhaps it is meant to be a word of caution. In our world, extremes are everywhere. Humans tend to draw lines to declare where we stand and to mark who is in and who is out. How do we know if we are being too salty or too bright, too bland or too dim?

Jesus says that salt can lose its saltiness. Salt only loses its saltiness when mixed with something else. When we stir together a recipe of nationalism, politics, and personal opinions with our journey of following Christ, we will lose our saltiness. Jesus also says that a light should not be hidden or dimmed. This isn't an invitation to shine a bright light of interrogation into the sinfulness of every person we meet, blinding them to the goodness of God. Rather, Jesus invites us to live in such a way that our light is revealed in the good deeds we do as we praise God in heaven.

To know if we are who Jesus says we are requires us to put our lives in the hands of the God who created us and loves us. If we are going to recognize the places where we have been too salty or too dim, we need the Holy Spirit to search us and know us. Jesus's declaration that we are salt and light is his way of telling us about our purpose.

In this season of preparation it is good to ask the question "What am I here for?" We will all hear different answers. We all have different callings. We are all directed by different God-given passions. What we all share is our calling to be the people of God. We follow a Savior who dwells with us, who challenged the self-righteous religious leaders of his day, who stood against the sinful systems of oppression, and who was ultimately crucified for it all. May we be directed by the Light of the world and not the powers, trends, or patterns of this world.

This Advent season, we are reminded that our hope is in the One who has told us we are the salt of the earth and the light of the world. May we allow the one who came in the gentleness of a baby to form us into the people of God's desire. May we fulfill our purpose.

FOR REFLECTION

Following Jesus is a journey. On this journey we can get off track. Think about the things that are most important to you and write them down. It might be family, work, country, or calling. As you pray, ask God to reveal to you whether you have lost your saltiness by mixing your relationship with God with other things. In prayer, consider where you may have been too salty or too dim. In hope, ask God to guide you.

SCRIPTURE READING

PSALM 119:105–112

Your word is a lamp before my feet and a light for my journey. I have sworn, and I fully mean it: I will keep your righteous rules. I have been suffering so much—LORD, make me live again according to your promise. Please, LORD, accept my spontaneous gifts of praise. Teach me your rules! Though my life is constantly in danger, I won't forget your Instruction. Though the wicked have set a trap for me, I won't stray from your precepts. Your laws are my possession forever because they are my heart's joy. I have decided to keep your statutes forever, every last one.

—PSALM 119:105–112

When I hear the first verse of our passage today two things happen in my mind. First, I start humming the old chorus "Thy Word." Second, I imagine myself in a forest with towering trees swaying in the dark night. Ferns decorate the pathway, and I am barefoot. My feet pad along the reddish-brown, dusty path, and in my hand is a lantern lit with a flame. The light illumines a small portion of the way in front of me. It feels like a romantic vision of another time and place, as though I am some character in a Jane Austen novel headed to a windswept beach.

The image of the psalm is not romantic, though. It is dramatic. There is suffering. There is the threat of death. There is danger. There are enemies. There are wicked people. There are traps. The psalmist isn't messing around in describing the trouble we can face in our lives. The path is neither smooth nor easy. There are challenges and dangers. Sometimes it feels like it is too dark to see. In that moment we need a light to guide us on the treacherous way.

The psalmist tells us that light is the Word of God— the Scriptures, the precepts, God's truth—that reveal the way we should go. This doesn't mean the Bible is a road map. To treat it so simply diminishes its true value. As followers of Christ we must be careful not to worship our Bibles but instead worship the One our Bible reveals. The light to our path isn't just having the Good Book in our backpack, or passages hidden in our hearts—though those are both important. The light to our path is the truth that God is with us. We know God, and God knows us. We trust God, and God partners with us. We love God, and God loves us. It is in this relationship that the way is lit before us.

It is dangerous to boil Scripture down to formulas. When we do that, we make our journey with God about transactions. No good, deep, rich relationship can be transactional. If the only reason I am trying to follow God's commandments is to get something for myself—even the good something of salvation—then I have missed the whole point. The psalmist declares a desire to be faithful to all of these things and to live as Scripture says *in order to* live in right relationship with God—not to make a deal with God. We need God's presence and truth for the journey. When we are walking in the difficult days, down the dangerous paths, it isn't going to cut it to have traded something for something else. No. We need a companion with us to light the way. We need the God of creation—God-with-us—to help us live according to the promise. Let God light your way today.

FOR REFLECTION OR DISCUSSION

1. Are there some particular places that feel difficult in your life? Where do you need God to light your way today?

_____

_____

_____

_____

_____

_____

_____

2. How has reading and knowing Scripture transformed your life?

_____

_____

_____

_____

_____

_____

The Zeal of the Lord

Thursday, December 2, 2021

SCRIPTURE READING

ISAIAH 9:1-7

The people walking in darkness have seen a great light. On those living in a pitch-dark land, light has dawned.

As on the day of Midian, you've shattered the yoke that burdened them, the staff on their shoulders, and the rod of their oppressor. Because every boot of the thundering warriors, and every garment rolled in blood will be burned, fuel for the fire. A child is born to us, a son is given to us, and authority will be on his shoulders. He will be named Wonderful Counselor, Mighty God, Eternal Father, Prince of Peace. There will be vast authority and endless peace for David's throne and for his kingdom, establishing and sustaining it with justice and righteousness now and forever. The zeal of the LORD of heavenly forces will do this.

—ISAIAH 9:2, 4-7

The best stories, movies, and sermons cause us to relate in some way to what we are seeing and hearing. Scripture is no different. There is great value in being able to see ourselves in the pages of the Bible. It helps us to internalize, to be transformed, to empathize, and more when we connect with what we read or see.

One way to connect with today's passage is to feel grateful that a light has dawned. We may think we've been walking in darkness for too long, and we praise

God for the morning and for the child—the son—that has been given to us. Many of us are probably used to reading this passage in just this way. What if we tried a different way to read this passage that removes ourselves from the center of the story?

If we were to look for the distressed, the people in darkness, those wearing a heavy yoke of oppression, those whose garments have been rolled in blood by the warriors that march on and on—whom would we find in our neighborhoods, our communities, our churches, and the world? If they are the ones who are rejoicing in the text, then whom might we be? When we only read ourselves as the oppressed, the ones in darkness, the ones needing that light to dawn, we are often blind to the oppression of others around us. We need a bigger vision. Lord, be a lamp to our feet!

That larger vision came for me as I sat around a table inside the razor wire of a state prison. I looked women in the eyes who had life experiences I couldn't comprehend. Yes, they had broken the law in various ways—that's why they were in that book club with me behind bars—but I saw how they had been broken by circumstances in their lives. One doesn't have to listen long to conversations in that punishing space to know that abuse, trauma, oppression, racism, and poverty have impacted the vast majority of the women who are incarcerated. You know who needs a light to dawn? They do. When I place the women I know who are in prison at the center of the scriptural text in Isaiah, the way I interpret the story told there changes.

Yes, I do need the light to dawn on my own darkness. Yes, I do need the child who is foretold to be my Prince of Peace. Yes, I do need the yoke of oppression broken. But when those things happen for me, they aren't just for me. Because a light has dawned on my own darkness, I now need to examine my own heart, my actions, my practices, my attitudes, the systems in which I am complicit—and allow the light to shine on the places where I am the one who brings darkness, oppression, and discord. Search me, God! Show me where I have not been who you have called me to be in this world! Take me out of the center of the story and reveal the sin, the habits, the blindness I have had to those walking in darkness around me. I have hope; may I share hope. I have light; may I share light.

FOR REFLECTION OR DISCUSSION

1. How does it make you feel to intentionally read Scripture
    from a different perspective—where you might not be the
    main character or even a protagonist? Discomfort is often
    a place where growth happens. Jot down your feelings and
    take a moment to ask God to help you grow as a disciple.

    _____

    _____

    _____

    _____

    _____

    _____

    _____

    _____

2. What is something you can do today to bring light to
    those around you?

    _____

    _____

    _____

    _____

    _____

    _____

    _____

    _____

    _____

Friday, December 3, 2021

SCRIPTURE READING

GENESIS 15:1-6

*But Abram said, "L*ORD *God, what can you possibly give me, since I still have no children? The head of my household is Eliezer, a man from Damascus." He continued, "Since you haven't given me any children, the head of my household will be my heir."*

*The L*ORD*'s word came immediately to him, "This man will not be your heir. Your heir will definitely be your very own biological child." Then he brought Abram outside and said, "Look up at the sky and count the stars if you think you can count them." He continued, "This is how many children you will have."*
—GENESIS 15:2-5

God brings hope when there appears to be no hope. That's what we find in today's text, where Abram has yet to receive the fulfillment of God's promise to him. Although I know this story well from multiple readings over the years, there is an interesting detail in it that I never really noticed before: when God takes Abram outside to remind him of the promise by looking at and trying to count the stars in the sky, what time of day is it? I always imagined the sandy hills dotted with scrub brush under a deep sapphire sky dotted with millions of tiny pinpricks of light. I have imagined Abram looking up and seeing those billions and billions of stars and feeling awe at the promise of God.

But, just a few sentences later in verse 17, we read that the sun sets. So, it's daytime in the earlier verses? Did God take Abram outside in the broad daylight and tell him to count the stars? If so, there would've been only one star visible—the sun. Now, of course, God could have given Abram heavenly vision. In the midst of the glaring sunshine of a day in the Middle East, God could certainly have shown Abram something beyond what he could have seen with his eyes—of course God can do that. But what if—because it is not perfectly clear here in the text—all Abram could see was the sun? Yet he had faith.

Whether it is the light of a heavenly vision that reveals multitudes of stars in the daylight, or it is the hot, glaring star we call the sun, what will we do with the promise? When we can't see the whole picture, what sort of disciples will we be?

This Advent season we celebrate the baby born in Bethlehem. We actually know that whole story—Jesus was born to a virgin, Mary. He grows up and teaches, preaches, heals, and challenges the religious and governmental authorities. The life he lives leads him to the cross, where he suffers a brutal death. On the third day he rises again and then ascends to sit at the right hand of God the Father. Our Messiah will come again. We know Jesus's life story, and we await his return. But what do we see today? Will we be people who trust, who believe, who follow—even though we weren't there? How will we respond without having firsthand experience? Will we be people who squint at the promise that doesn't look like the starry sky but still walk with God? Will we follow our Lord as we await his return? Will we be the light to the nations that Abraham's descendants were called to be in a world that desperately needs a godly vision?

We prefer the godly vision. We prefer the promise of billions and trillions and more. But what if God is asking us to go out in broad daylight and count the stars that we see? It doesn't seem like much. *Is God making fun of us?* we might wonder. *Is this really it, God? One?* Will we have faith in the God who makes unlikely promises to unlikely people, and allow his vision to be born in us? I hope we will.

FOR REFLECTION OR DISCUSSION

1. What is something you are struggling to trust God with?
    How can Abraham's faith help to shape your faith today?

    _____

    _____

    _____

    _____

    _____

    _____

2. Do you feel like you are squinting at the sun when you
    would rather see trillions of stars? Write a prayer of trust
    to God, putting your hope in God's plans.

    _____

    _____

    _____

    _____

    _____

    _____

    _____

    _____

    _____

    _____

    _____

    _____

    _____

Saturday, December 4, 2021

SCRIPTURE READING

1 PETER 1:3-9

*Although you've never seen him, you love him. Even
though you don't see him now, you trust him and so
rejoice with a glorious joy that is too much for words.
You are receiving the goal of your faith: your salvation.*
—1 PETER 1:8-9

As we come to the end of this first week of Advent, the
words of Peter are a beautiful place to sit and reflect
on the hope we have in Christ. Remember, this isn't
merely a time to celebrate the first coming of Christ
as a baby in a manger. It is also a time to wait expectantly for Christ's return. We look back *and* we look
forward as we live and experience the present.

The end of the passage in today's text has captivated
me. I wasn't there at the manger, and I don't know
what it will be like when Jesus returns—yet I trust.
Why? How? Do you ever ask yourself this question?
*Why do I believe this wild story about the life, death,
and resurrection of Jesus told to us by Scripture?* If
we can't explain how it is going to be at the end of all
things, how can we trust in God? The reality Peter
writes about is the result of those who have said, "I
offer my life to you, Lord" (Psalm 25:1).

Those who love and follow Jesus have been a torch
in my darkness. Fellow sojourners have been just the

right amount of salt and light to help me taste and see that God is good. Patient saints have walked with me on the path and shown that the light for our way is the Light of the world—Jesus. Sanctified travelers have helped me squint up at the sun and trust the promise. This doesn't mean I worship those people. It means their light has given me vision for what I could not see on my own. Their lanterns of faith lit my path, and I came to see that my companion all along was Jesus.

As I think about each of these people, my heart is full of joy. My prayer is that we share the light with others, inviting them to come to the manger and see the Savior of the world. My desire is that we will have the courage to stand against the darkness of destructive systems of oppression. May we shine Jesus's light of truth in places that have been allowed to harm and destroy for too long. My hope is that we will shine the way for each other and for the world as we await the glorious return of our Lord.

Light a candle. You are receiving the goal of your faith: your salvation.

FOR REFLECTION OR DISCUSSION

1. Reflect on the theme of hope from this first week of Advent. List some ways you have felt hopeful.

_____

_____

_____

_____

_____

_____

_____

2. Take some time to reflect on ways you saw hope and brought hope in your family, church, and community this week.

_____

_____

_____

_____

_____

_____

_____

_____

_____

_____

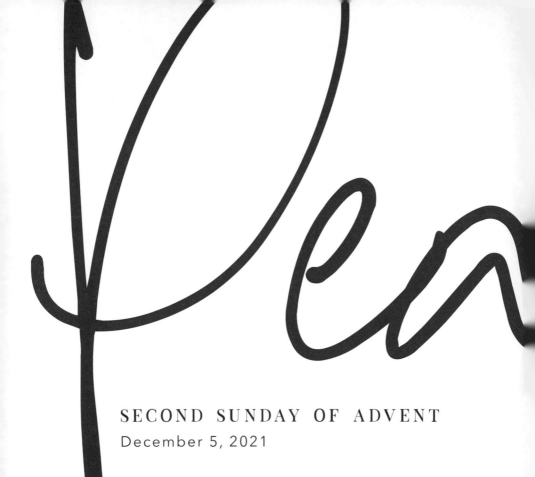

SECOND SUNDAY OF ADVENT

December 5, 2021

SCRIPTURE READING

LUKE 3:1-6

John went throughout the region of the Jordan River, calling for people to be baptized to show that they were changing their hearts and lives and wanted God to forgive their sins. This is just as it was written in the scroll of the words of Isaiah the prophet, "A voice crying out in the wilderness: 'Prepare the way for the Lord; make his paths straight. Every valley will be filled, and every mountain and hill will be leveled. The crooked will be made straight and the rough places made smooth. All humanity will see God's salvation.'"

—LUKE 3:3-6

John the Baptist is not the first person to come to mind when thinking about peace. He might not even be the tenth. His ministry was strange, right down to the clothes he wore, and his message was confrontational: "Repent! Change! Confess! Be baptized!" The disruption John brings is echoed in the Isaiah text that is quoted in our passage for today. John's ministry certainly was not peaceful. Rough places becoming smooth requires hard, grinding work. Valleys being filled and mountains leveled evokes violent images of surging and quaking earth. Crooked becoming straight is tedious and challenging work.

So why is this our text on a day we are called to observe peace? Shouldn't we instead have quiet waters and green pastures? Isn't this a time for us to consider the rest that God offers all of us? What about ceasing war? Why are we reading about John the Baptist? John's father, Zechariah, sang in praise to God about the birth of his son: "Because of our God's deep compassion, the dawn from heaven will break upon us, to give light to those who are sitting in darkness and in the shadow of death, to guide us on the path of peace" (Luke 1:78–80).

The path toward peace isn't easy. The path toward peace isn't smooth. The path toward peace is risky, takes courage, and challenges the broken realities of the world. For peace to come, we must get to the hard work of aligning a world made crooked by sin with the straight paths of the kingdom of God. For peace to come, there is creative work that makes valleys of despair into mountaintops of hope. For peace to come, there is repetitive work that sands away injustice to bring about the smoothness of equity. Without the work, without the challenge, and without upsetting the status quo, peace will not come.

One of my favorite ways John the Baptist talks about his ministry is when he says in John 3:30, "He [Jesus] must increase and I must decrease." This really is the way of peace. When you and I strive and work and manipulate and attempt to make ourselves greater, there is no peace. Rather, we feel smaller, weaker, suspicious, and fearful. Our quest for control, power, or position leaves our lives in turmoil. John's invitation to change our lives is an invitation to follow his example. Jesus increases, and all that stuff I tried to do to keep my own peace—well, that decreases.

This is both a choice and a promise. When we choose to heed the call of John—*Repent! Change your life!*— we choose to lay ourselves aside and allow the Holy Spirit to shape us in the image of Christ. This doesn't mean we have no personality or distinctive qualities. It means we become who we were meant to be. Our personalities are made holy. Our passions are transformed. Our imaginations are sanctified. I am still me, but it is Christ in me who perfects my purpose. As I daily make this choice, God promises that those rough places will become smooth, the low places raised, and the crooked straightened. I don't do this by working extra hard. God does it, through love, in great mercy and grace. We decrease, Christ increases.

FOR REFLECTION OR DISCUSSION

1. What is the most peaceful place, experience, or moment you have had in your life?

   _____

   _____

   _____

   _____

   _____

2. How would you describe the difference between keeping peace and making peace?

   _____

   _____

   _____

   _____

   _____

3. Is there something that needs to decrease in you so Christ can increase? If so, what are some steps you can take to choose to decrease and also to receive the grace of God to do this?

   _____

   _____

   _____

   _____

   _____

SCRIPTURE READING

LUKE 13:18–21

Jesus asked, "What is God's kingdom like? To what can I compare it? It's like a mustard seed that someone took and planted in a garden. It grew and developed into a tree and the birds in the sky nested in its branches." Again he said, "To what can I compare God's kingdom? It's like yeast, which a woman took and hid in a bushel of wheat flour until the yeast had worked its way through the whole."

—LUKE 13:18–21

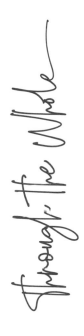

It is easy for us to judge from the outside. "Don't judge a book by its cover," we might say to admonish this kind of behavior—but it's hard not to, isn't it? And not just books. We judge people by how they look all the time. We judge their worth based on what they own, how they dress, what they drive, how their teeth look, and whether their fingernails are clean. We judge people by their "covers" all the time.

Jesus wants to undo this kind of thinking. He knows our human tendency is to judge what is good as bad and what is bad as good. This is one of the reasons Jesus became incarnate in the manner in which he did. We like to believe a ruler in a palace is going to save us. We judge their position, power, wealth, and rhetoric as good. We put our trust in human beings and are all too often mistaken. That leader we lifted up will not bring the peace they promise. If Jesus had been born to a ruling family, to a palace—that would have made sense to our judging minds. But Jesus instead came to a humble virgin. Jesus was born in a stable and laid in a manger. Jesus was greeted by people on the fringes—shepherds and foreigners. Jesus was materially poor and had no place to rest his head. This tells us we can't judge God's kingdom and God's way of doing things with our usual metrics.

John the Baptist didn't come up with "he must increase and I must decrease" (John 3:30) on his own. This is the way of Jesus. He emptied, humbled, and subjected himself to us. He chose to decrease to heal our poor judgment and our sin that leads to our own oppression. But it wasn't enough to embody all of that. We are painfully stuck in our ways. Jesus had to teach this concept to his disciples again and again and again.

The kingdom of God isn't like the kingdoms of this world. In Luke he says, "What is God's kingdom like? To what can I compare it?" These simple questions in today's text actually point to the more complex reality of our propensity to judge wrongly. Jesus has to look around carefully to draw on what is in the world to help us all see what God's kingdom is *really* like.

Mustard seeds and yeast are two of the things Jesus lands on to help change how we judge what really matters—a tiny seed and a tiny leavening agent. Don't judge a seed by its hull! Don't judge a catalyst by its proportions! That seed, when planted and nurtured, will grow. That yeast, when mixed carefully into the flour and water, will blossom. The seed becomes a place for others to gather. The yeast becomes bread that can be shared with a neighbor. What looks small and worthless transforms to bring life, value, beauty, and sustenance.

As we engage in the downward journey to allow Christ to increase in us, our lives actually take on more value and purpose. When we follow in the ways of the world and seek power, position, and prestige, trying to make ourselves increase, we will find ourselves listless and empty. In the hands of our King, our lives become what they were always meant to be. The one who has come and is coming again offers true peace when we surrender to him.

FOR REFLECTION OR DISCUSSION

1. Has there been a time in your life when something very small made a difference? Take a moment and reflect on that experience and thank God for that gift.

_____

_____

_____

_____

_____

_____

_____

_____

2. Is there someone in your social sphere who is often over-looked or (mis)judged? What can you do to create space for God's kingdom to flourish in that person?

_____

_____

_____

_____

_____

_____

_____

_____

_____

_____

_____

SCRIPTURE READING

JOHN 6:1-14

Jesus looked up and saw the large crowd coming toward him. He asked Philip, "Where will we buy food to feed these people?" Jesus said this to test him, for he already knew what he was going to do.

Philip replied, "More than half a year's salary worth of food wouldn't be enough for each person to have even a little bit."

One of his disciples, Andrew, Simon Peter's brother, said, "A youth here has five barley loaves and two fish. But what good is that for a crowd like this?"
—JOHN 6:5-9

My youngest son is a whirlwind. He is creative, adventurous, easily distracted, and courageously tries new things. This often means he makes giant messes. When he was small he would bring out all of his blocks, books, cars, and anything else that caught his eye. When it was time to clean up he would stretch out his hands, look down at them, and then look up at me or my husband and say, "But my tiny little hands!"

It was hard not to laugh. I would say, "Your tiny little hands made this mess! They are more than capable of cleaning it up," and we would all work together to conquer the task.

Jesus asks Philip in our passage today, "Where will we buy food to feed these people?" The text tells us a large crowd is coming their way.

Philip's response is much like my son's. It's almost like he looked down at his hands and up at Jesus and said, "Have you seen my tiny little hands?"

It does seem a little bit ridiculous that Jesus is asking the disciples to figure out how to feed this large crowd. They don't have anything! They have given up so much! How could Jesus expect more from them?

I don't know if Andrew has great faith in Jesus or if he is trying to prove how impossible this whole predicament has become. Whatever his motivation, he brings a child who has a simple lunch to Jesus. There are five loaves made from barley and two fish to feed the whole crowd. In the face of a hungry and harassed multitude this seems silly, impossible, and maybe even rude. Yet, in the pattern that is oft repeated, Jesus took it, blessed it, broke it, and gave it. The willingness of the young man to offer what he had became a blessing no one could have imagined. In Jesus's hands, what we have is enough.

The question for us today as we seek peace is: What is in our hands, and whose hand do we hold? To pursue peace, we need to have one holding onto Jesus and the other outstretched toward the world around us. When I live with one hand up and one hand out, I will have peace and make peace. If I try to hold Jesus's hand but keep my other hand behind my back, I can miss out on God's desire for myself and those around me. If I try to hold one hand out and keep the one that should be in Jesus's hand in my pocket, my life will always be limited by my own imagination for what is possible. When we stretch out one hand toward the world and hold the hand of Jesus with the other, what we have is multiplied.

This might sound good to us, but we might also be secretly looking down at our hands and up into the face of God and out into the faces of those around us and think, *But my tiny little hands!* Jesus, who was born in a manger, Jesus, the Messiah who will return, is asking us, "What will you do to make a difference in the lives of those who are physically and spiritually hungry all around you?" He asks us this question already knowing what he wants to do. Will we hold his hand, giving him what we have? Will we extend our hands to those in need around us? When we do, our lives will be filled with peace because loving God and loving people are what we were made for.

FOR REFLECTION OR DISCUSSION

1. Jesus already knew what he wanted to do when he asked Philip how they could feed the crowd (John 6:6). Reflect on what this means in your life as you extend your hands to God and to the world.

   _____

   _____

   _____

   _____

   _____

   _____

2. What is a skill, a passion, or a talent you have that you could offer to God and to the world?

   _____

   _____

   _____

   _____

   _____

   _____

   _____

   _____

   _____

   _____

Wednesday, December 8, 2021

SCRIPTURE READING

EPHESIANS 2:14-22

Christ is our peace. He made both Jews and Gentiles into one group. With his body, he broke down the barrier of hatred that divided us.

When he came, he announced the good news of peace to you who were far away from God and to those who were near. We both have access to the Father through Christ by the one Spirit.

Christ is building you into a place where God lives through the Spirit.

—EPHESIANS 2:14, 17-18, 22

My husband and I pastored in a town that was home to a religiously conservative church. The members of this community believe it is the "one true church." These Christians engage in business in the communities where they live, but they disavow many of the practices of their neighbors. Women wear dresses and cover their hair, which they rarely cut. Men grow beards and drive trucks that can't be two-toned in color or have radios. They sing without instruments in their churches and engage in the practices of confession and Communion once a year.

We became acquainted with a family from this church at a coffee shop in our town. The father of the family was in the process of being expelled from his church. Since my husband was often to be found in the coffee shop with his Bible while he worked on sermons, they struck up a friendship. To be expelled is very serious. It requires an investigation into the behavior of the member in question, and after that they hold a public trial and a congregational vote. If the congregation votes to expel, the expelled member can't take Communion and must separate from the church. It also means they can come to family meals, but they have to eat in the kitchen, separately from the rest of the family.

We prayed with the family over the weeks through the investigation and leading up to the trial. Our friendship deepened as we supported this family. On the night of the vote, the charges were read against our friend. One elder stood up and said, as evidence that our friend should be expelled, "He loves Jesus more than he loves the church."

When I heard those words I began to weep. Isn't that what we all would want? Isn't this a true and deep relationship with the living God? I love the church. I *need* the church. But, ultimately, I must fix my eyes upon Jesus. He is who I must follow. If our churches are helping this to be true in our lives, praise God! But churches can begin to believe *they* are the savior, the judge, or even God. It isn't always outside the church that dividing walls are built. Ungodly division can be found in the very place meant to embody the One who tears down such walls.

Paul writes of the work of Christ, who is our peace; Jesus breaks down the dividing wall of hostility. We know there are walls that are against us in the wider world. There are walls that have been erected to stand in opposition to the good news of Jesus Christ. There are also walls you and I have helped build. Brick by brick we have built up anger and hostility. Brick by brick we have said one side of the wall is better than the other. Brick by brick we have not been peacemakers but builders of dissension. Lord, help us.

This is a perfect time for us to search our hearts, to remember the peace that was declared at Jesus's birth, the peace that was part of his ministry, the peace that his life, death, and resurrection bring, and the peace that will come when he returns. Christ's peace knocks down division and brings unity. That doesn't mean people come to see it our way—it means we love Jesus so much we see it his way. With my eyes on Jesus, I see you as a beloved child of God, I see my neighbor as a beloved child of God, I see those who are my enemies as beloved children of God—I see all people, everywhere, as beloved children of God.

Our friend modeled for us what seeking peace meant. Although a wall of hostility was built against him, he continued to demonstrate love to his family and friends. I don't know what the future will hold for him, but he and his family continue to seek peace. May we keep our eyes fixed on Jesus no matter the cost. May we decrease so Christ can increase. This will eventually cause hostility to crumble and the peace of Christ to reign.

FOR REFLECTION OR DISCUSSION

1. How do you need Christ to break down dividing walls of hostility in your life?

    _____

    _____

    _____

    _____

    _____

    _____

    _____

    _____

2. Our text tells us that God has brought us near. In what ways can this understanding of God's desire for us change how you treat others today?

    _____

    _____

    _____

    _____

    _____

    _____

    _____

    _____

    _____

SCRIPTURE READING

HABAKKUK 3:17-19

Though the fig tree does not bud and there are no grapes on the vines, though the olive crop fails and the fields produce no food, though there are no sheep in the pen and no cattle in the stalls, yet I will rejoice in the LORD, I will be joyful in God my Savior.
—HABAKKUK 3:17-18, NIV

As we meet Habakkuk today, things are not going well for the prophet or for God's people. The prophet wants justice, and God is not delivering. The prophet wants vengeance, and God is silent. The prophet doesn't understand God's ways and wants God to act. The enemies have been allowed to win for too long. C'mon, God, do something!

When things aren't going the way we expect we have many different options. One way forward is to practice seeking God's presence in the midst of our disappointment and frustration. This is real for Habakkuk and God's people. Things really are falling apart. Completely. No food, no crops, no animals—nothing is left.

In the ancient world, many people worshiped fertility gods. You worshiped Baal to have children, crops, animals, and harvest. When those things didn't happen it was easy to assume the gods must be mad at you. This culture, of course, crept into the worship of God's people.

When things didn't go the way they expected, they saw it as punishment and wondered what they could do to appease God in the way of their idol-worshiping neighbors.

The prophet Habakkuk believes there is something different to do. We don't have to beat ourselves up, blame God, or try harder when things fall apart. Instead, we simply need to draw near to God. Habakkuk gives us two words that can help us practice seeking God's presence when it feels like God is far away: "though" and "yet."

"Though the fig tree does not bud . . . yet I will rejoice" (3:17, 18, NIV). Though everything around me is a mess, yet I will praise God. Though it seems like I am a failure, yet I will rejoice in the Lord. Though everyone believes I've done something wrong, yet I will trust the one who will lift me up. Though I feel lost and afraid, yet I will lean on God. Though and yet. When the world is in chaos, when everywhere we step feels like cascading rocks that will throw us off a cliff, praising God will give God the space in our pain and suffering to place us on the high, strong mountains, where he won't let our feet slip.

The beauty of this season is the reminder that God came near. God is with us—Emmanuel! It doesn't always *feel* like God is near, but in the incarnation we can *know* the depths of God's love and presence in our lives. *Though* we don't feel, *yet* we will praise. This is a pathway to peace for us in times that feel anything but peaceful. Though we have trouble, yet we will praise. And in the praise, God will draw near.

FOR REFLECTION OR DISCUSSION

1. Reflecting on your life, your pain, your frustrations, and your doubt, construct your own though/yet statements.

_____

_____

_____

_____

_____

_____

_____

_____

2. Have you been afraid to voice your true feelings to God? Habakkuk wasn't! What might you need to tell God if you really believed you could be honest?

_____

_____

_____

_____

_____

_____

_____

_____

Friday, December 10, 2021

SCRIPTURE READING

EXODUS 16

The whole Israelite community complained against Moses and Aaron in the desert. The Israelites said to them, "Oh, how we wish that the LORD had just put us to death while we were still in the land of Egypt. There we could sit by the pots cooking meat and eat our fill of bread. Instead, you've brought us out into this desert to starve this whole assembly to death."

Then the LORD said to Moses, "I'm going to make bread rain down from the sky for you. The people will go out each day and gather just enough for that day. In this way, I'll test them to see whether or not they follow my Instruction."

The Israelite people called it manna. It was like coriander seed, white, and tasted like honey wafers.

The Israelites ate manna for forty years, until they came to a livable land. They ate manna until they came to the border of the land of Canaan.
—EXODUS 16:2-4, 31, 35

Wandering in the wilderness was not the plan of the Hebrew people when they were freed from slavery. They cried out in their oppression, and God heard them, but shortly after their freedom, they longed to go back to Egypt. Why? The text tells us that at least they had good food to eat while they were slaves. It is easy to look at this story and think we would never be like this! *I would rather be free than worry about filling my belly. I would eat anything if my bondage and my chains were broken.* We might imagine these things to be true, but we also might be wrong.

The issue for the Israelites was that they were willing to trade their freedom for the security of not having to trust God in the unknown. The Israelites thought they would rather deal with what they could understand and predict than wait on the Lord. The people wanted a pot of hot soup instead of a relationship with the living God. Are we so different from the Israelites in the wilderness?

God, of course, does provide for the people. It might not be what they expect, but God takes care of them. Manna and quail are given for their food. One of the fascinating things about the gift of manna is that no one can take more than they needed. They *could* take more, but it won't last. God didn't give excess—God provided what the people needed for life.

In a world driven by consuming more and more, manna doesn't make a lot of sense to us. In a society that seeks to convince us we will never be satisfied, manna seems strange. In a culture that celebrates those who have excess, manna is a message we need to heed. Over-consumption does not lead to peace. Having more than enough does not satisfy. Hoarding leads to fear and suspicion, not a flourishing life. God was teaching the people in the desert the important lesson of reliance. When we come to understand that everything we have is God's, then we will change how we buy, consume, and give. When I think all of this is *mine*, I will try to fill my belly, my barns, and my storage units to try to fill my soul. Manna was always enough. When we trust in God, we will have enough.

This kind of thinking can lead to problems for us as Christians. In the face of hungry kids in our communities, starving people across the globe, and economies that exploit the weak, we need to be very careful not to preach a message to the poor of trusting in God while we stock our pantries, throw out good food, or make purchases that harm them. If we have more than enough, we ought to share what we have. If God's peace is *shalom*—a flourishing for all people and the earth—then the message isn't, "Have more faith, and you will have enough!" The message is instead, "I have much, and I will share so we both have enough."

Spiritual manna is a reminder that nothing but knowing and loving God will satisfy or bring true peace. Physical manna is a reminder that we are part of God's family and should seek the peace and flourishing of our neighbors. Thanks be to God that we are provided for! May we respond by providing peace, *shalom*, and well-being for others.

FOR REFLECTION OR DISCUSSION

1. How have you seen God provide for you?

_____

_____

_____

_____

_____

_____

_____

_____

_____

_____

2. How can you use the provisions you have to be a blessing to someone this holiday season?

_____

_____

_____

_____

_____

_____

_____

_____

_____

_____

Saturday, December 11, 2021

SCRIPTURE READING

MATTHEW 13:1-9

He said many things to them in parables: "A farmer went out to scatter seed. As he was scattering seed, some fell on the path, and birds came and ate it. Other seed fell on rocky ground where the soil was shallow. They sprouted immediately because the soil wasn't deep. But when the sun came up, it scorched the plants, and they dried up because they had no roots. Other seed fell among thorny plants. The thorny plants grew and choked them. Other seed fell on good soil and bore fruit, in one case a yield of one hundred to one, in another case a yield of sixty to one, and in another case a yield of thirty to one."

—MATTHEW 13:3-8

I want to have a garden. I want to be able to eat the produce I grow. I want my table to be filled with the bounty of the earth that has been tended by my very own hands. There is something special about planting a seedling and, later, picking and eating a fruit or vegetable. If you have ever grown anything—whether for necessity, for beauty, or for the joy of it—you know that there are requirements for a successful crop or bouquet. The soil matters.

In this parable a farmer is sowing seed all over the place. There is no kind of soil that doesn't receive the seed. This is important for us to know. God, as the farmer, doesn't discriminate about where the seed gets sown. God sows seeds of love, grace, forgiveness, and life everywhere, at all times. God seeks our peace, our *shalom*, our flourishing. This is such a hopeful message, and it is also a directive for us to sow the good news wherever we go: God is good! God loves you! God has true life for you!

But that isn't the only message in this parable. The other message is that the soil matters. God may be a gracious and generous farmer, but we are obligated to participate with God in our own formation. You and I have a responsibility to tend the soil of our hearts so that the seeds God is planting will blossom and grow and produce a harvest. Too often we see our job as tending the soil of the hearts of others. "Here," we might say, "let me pull that weed out for you!" Or, "Let me lend you this tool to dig out all of those terrible rocks!" We are convinced that helping others be ready for the seed is good work.

Jesus's interpretation of this parable is telling, though. In this season of preparation it is important for us to take a look inside. Although we have a responsibility to the world around us to dig up the weeds of oppression and injustice, and we should work with others to be the people God has called us to be—if the soil of my own heart is not constantly tilled and tended, are the seeds of God's kingdom able to grow in me? If I am so busy attending to everyone and everything else instead of my own heart, what will happen to me or even through me?

We are called to be people who rest in the peace of the kingdom of God that has come and is coming. We are people invited into a relationship with the Creator of the universe, who also invites us to be God's friend. We are meant to address our personal relationship with God—but never at the expense of neglecting our relationship with our neighbors. We don't focus only on one; we are called to love God *and* love people. Tending the soil of our hearts prepares us to love our neighbors well. As we love our neighbors, we demonstrate our love for God. As we love God we will, without question, love our neighbors.

Is the soil of my heart a place where God's peace can take root? Is the soil of my heart a place where God's peace can grow into plants that bear kingdom fruit? Is the soil of my heart a place where God's peace can grow into justice and mercy? God is sowing seeds. Is the soil of my heart ready?

FOR REFLECTION OR DISCUSSION

1. One of the questions John Wesley liked to ask in his
    small groups was, "How is it with your soul?" Take a
    moment to consider and write down your answer to this
    probing question.

    _____

    _____

    _____

    _____

    _____

    _____

    _____

    _____

    _____

2. What is a spiritual practice you think could help you as
    you seek to have a heart ready for the peace of God? Why
    do you think it would be helpful?

    _____

    _____

    _____

    _____

    _____

    _____

    _____

    _____

THIRD SUNDAY OF ADVENT

December 12, 2021

SCRIPTURE READING

LUKE 3:7-18

Then John said to the crowds who came to be baptized by him, "You children of snakes! Who warned you to escape from the angry judgment that is coming soon? Produce fruit that shows you have changed your hearts and lives."

The crowds asked him, "What then should we do?"
—LUKE 3:7-8a, 10

Joy is deep and abiding, rich and rewarding. Joy is a well that does not run dry when trouble comes. Joy is our theme for the third week of Advent.

Today we again find John the Baptist speaking hard and challenging words to the people who have come out to hear his message. He points out their sin, manipulation, and harm of one another. Hungry for true life, the people who are gathered near him do not bristle at being called snakes. Instead, they respond with a repeated question: "What should we do?"

To be blameless at the judgment, what should we do? To produce good fruit, what should we do? To stay rooted, what should we do? In our particular circumstance, what should we do?

Asking and answering this question can help us find joy. The reason this question is so important is that it gets to the heart of things. What we do helps us become who we are meant to be in the kingdom of God. This combination of doing and becoming is a journey of joy that will change everything for us.

John challenges the people to engage in actions that demonstrate care for others. Give clothing and food to those in need, do not cheat people, be sure not to harass anyone. This is what he tells the crowd to do after preaching a message about repentance. At the heart of what John is communicating is a distinct challenge to the way the world wants us to live. The siren song of our culture is consumption. Consume more, and you will be fulfilled. Consume more, and you will be happy. Consume more, and you will have worth. When we allow ourselves to be entranced by this song, we will never find true joy. There is never enough when we view the world, possessions, and people as objects to consume.

There are many good things to consume during the Advent and Christmas seasons. Good food will be shared around tables. Thoughtful gifts will be given to those we love. Church choirs will fill our hearts and minds with the beauty of the season, and children's Christmas programs will warm our hearts and make us laugh. The lights and decorations will be a feast for our eyes as we bask in the beauty of this time of year. There is nothing inherently wrong with any of this. What is wrong is the failure to ask in the midst of this time, "What shall we do?"

May we hear the words of John the Baptist—the one who prepared the way for our Lord and Savior, Jesus Christ. Share with those in need. Feed those who are hungry. Treat people the way you want to be treated. Do not harm your neighbor. Be grateful. When we turn toward the baby in the manger and when we look forward to our returning King our actions, enabled by grace, will change us and the world around us. We must be careful not to behave in these ways only during the holiday season. John calls the people at the river—and us today—to a fundamentally new life that is different from the way we have been living and different from the way others would encourage us to live. We are invited into this new way of *doing* so we can *become* people of joy. This doing involves sharing, giving, respecting, honoring, and caring for people around us. Joy comes when I hold what I have lightly—my possessions, my position, my finances—so I can give it freely. Joy comes in truly showing love to the other.

What shall we do? We shall find joy.

FOR REFLECTION OR DISCUSSION

1. What brings you the greatest joy during this time of year and why?

_____

_____

_____

_____

_____

_____

_____

_____

_____

_____

_____

_____

_____

_____

_____

_____

2. Reflecting on your own life, how would you answer the
    question, "What should we do?"

    _____

    _____

    _____

    _____

    _____

    _____

    _____

    _____

    _____

    _____

    _____

3. What is one practical thing you can do this week to an-
    swer this question and find joy in your own life?

    _____

    _____

    _____

    _____

    _____

    _____

    _____

    _____

    _____

    _____

They Left Their Nets and Followed Him

SCRIPTURE READING

MATTHEW 4:12-22

As Jesus walked alongside the Galilee Sea, he saw two brothers, Simon, who is called Peter, and Andrew, throwing fishing nets into the sea, because they were fishermen. "Come, follow me," he said, "and I'll show you how to fish for people." Right away, they left their nets and followed him. Continuing on, he saw another set of brothers, James the son of Zebedee and his brother John. They were in a boat with Zebedee their father repairing their nets. Jesus called them and immediately they left the boat and their father and followed him.
—MATTHEW 4:18-22

It is often startling to us when we read the way Jesus's disciples just up and leave what they were doing to follow him. I wonder how I would have felt as a mother in this situation if I had two sons who were called by a religious teacher, and they just dropped everything and followed. In many ways it makes very little sense. How will they support themselves? Who is this teacher? Is this the best path for them when they could learn the family business? Why are they so eager to go? What will the future hold for them?

I have learned in my own life that the call of God can be startling. Sometimes when God calls and we respond, the people around us don't understand. There are moments when we are obedient to God and the path is not at all clear before us. That doesn't mean we should not obey. When I was young I sensed a call to be a missionary. Whenever I heard a missionary speak I was certain that was what I was supposed to do—but I did not want to be a missionary! It didn't line up with my own vision for my life. How could I do the things I wanted to do if I followed that call?

Things changed for me when I was fourteen and my family went to Romania and spent time with missionaries. My eyes were opened to a different reality, my heart was softened to God's call, and I responded with a firm yes to God, which led to more opportunities to say yes—for God's call isn't just a one-time event! Soon after I accepted this path for my life, I felt a whisper in my heart that God wanted me to preach. I had never heard a woman preach. Was God really calling me to that? I said yes again. I want to say yes every time I feel God calling.

Jesus is calling all of us, inviting us into the only life that brings true joy—one of following him. If it had been my boys on the beach that day, I hope they would have immediately dropped their nets. I hope I have raised them in such a way that the whisper of God to go, or to come, or to speak, or be silent is one they will heed. It would give me immense joy for them to drop everything and follow. If that is how I feel as an earthly mother, imagine how our heavenly Father feels when we follow. Imagine the joy God experiences as we enter into the good things God has for us.

This season is filled with joy in family gatherings, joy in giving gifts, joy in new beginnings. May we find joy in what is lasting and eternal and real this Advent season. Is God calling you to something today? Are you having a hard time saying yes? Does it feel like those around you are questioning whether it's the right thing to do? Hear the voice of Emmanuel—God with us—say to you today, "Come and follow!" When Jesus calls, drop your nets and follow. It is the most joyous journey you will ever go on.

FOR REFLECTION OR DISCUSSION

1. What is something you have felt, or are feeling, God is calling you to do? What has been your response to God's invitation?

_____

_____

_____

_____

_____

2. Why is it difficult for us to drop everything to follow Jesus?

_____

_____

_____

_____

_____

Tuesday, December 14, 2021

SCRIPTURE READING

MICAH 6:8

He has told you, human one, what is good and what the
Lord requires from you: to do justice, embrace faithful
love, and walk humbly with your God.
—MICAH 6.8

We all need to order our lives in one way or another.
Some people hang calendars on the wall to keep track
of what is happening. Some use digital planners to
keep track of to-do lists. We can set reminders on our
computers or phones that help us know what is happening next week, next month, or ten minutes from
now. I don't know very many people who don't seek
some sort of order to the things they have to do in life.

The prophet Micah has multiple lists, reminders,
and activities he addresses with God's people. Micah
lists the sins of the people. They have built idols and
worshiped them. They have oppressed and trampled
the weak. They have sought their own gain with no
care for God or neighbor. This is a brutal list. Micah
also lists the reactions of God to this behavior. God
will melt mountains like wax, God will be a witness
against the people who have behaved in this way, God
will destroy cities. In short, God will hold the people
accountable for their choices.

Consequences are real. We learn this from a young age. The consequence for God's people—for their disobedience, for their exploitation of others, for their idolatry, and for their violence—is that they themselves will be destroyed. The consequence for violence is more violence. But Micah reminds the people it doesn't have to be this way! There is a time coming, he declares to them, when there will be no more war. There is a time coming when nations will gather to worship the one true God. There is a time coming when God's peace will reign. This will be a time of great joy! This joy is revealed to us in another list given to us by Micah. To be in right relationship with God and with one another requires something of us. Get out your planner, your calendar, or your phone and jot it down: do justice, embrace faithful love, and walk humbly with your God. That's it. That's the list.

Today, may we ask the God who loves us and who has saved us to empower us by grace to live in this way. What should we do? Keep this list before you when you write out your daily to-do list, fill in squares on your calendar, or set up your daily reminders. Let the Micah 6:8 list guide your interactions with your family, friends, coworkers, and strangers you meet. As God's grace enables us to live in this way the world will become a better reflection of the kingdom. As we invite God to help us live justly, mercifully, and humbly, true joy will come. Let's add it to our to-do list.

FOR DISCUSSION OR REFLECTION

1. Have you thought of joy coming from being just, merciful, and humble before? Why or why not?

_____

_____

_____

_____

_____

_____

_____

2. Look over your schedule for tomorrow or your calendar for the month. What are some ways you can be more just, merciful, and humble in the midst of the upcoming activities and events in your life?

_____

_____

_____

_____

_____

_____

_____

_____

_____

Whoever Does the Will of My Father

Wednesday, December 15, 2021

SCRIPTURE READING

MATTHEW 12:46–50

Jesus replied, "Who is my mother? Who are my brothers?" He stretched out his hand toward his disciples and said, "Look, here are my mother and my brothers. Whoever does the will of my Father who is in heaven is my brother, sister, and mother."
—MATTHEW 12:48–50

Family can be so complicated, and at this time of year the pain of broken families is acute. Some members of our family won't be at the table this year because they have died. Some members of our family won't be at the Christmas party because they don't come anymore. Some members of our family won't be at the Christmas Eve service because they gave up on church a long time ago. Some members of our family won't be at Christmas breakfast because of divorce. Maybe "some members" describes you this year. Maybe you've been uninvited, or neglected, or you can't make it this year. Sometimes our family circumstances make joy feel far away and impossible to come by.

Jesus has some fascinating things to say about family that might surprise us. In our text for today, Jesus was in the middle of teaching the people when his mother and brothers came to speak to him. The crowd expected him to accommodate their request, and to be honest, many of us expect the same thing from Jesus in this passage—but Jesus used this as a teaching moment. He didn't turn everyone away so he could talk to his family. Instead, he redefined what family is.

In the kingdom of God, family might be the crew you are born into, but it might not be. In Jesus's definition of family, it has more to do with how we live our lives than with who makes up our genealogy. When we follow Jesus, our family should grow to be much bigger than we expected. Jesus's definition means we don't sequester in our homes with people whose last names match ours. We have all been grafted into God's family.

In a season that is filled with family gatherings, may you be reminded that you belong to a bigger family than you might have imagined. If you are blessed with a family that brings you great joy, remember those who don't have that gift and draw them into your fold. If you have the pain of a broken family that has brought nothing but sorrow, remember that you have been adopted into the loving family of God. For all of us, may we find deep joy in being obedient to our Savior—the baby in the manger, the King who reigns, and the Lord who will come again. It is so good to be part of his family.

FOR REFLECTION OR DISCUSSION

1. What feelings come to mind when you think of Jesus's definition of family?

2. Who in your life needs family? How can you help to create a spiritual family for those who are struggling?

Thursday, December 16, 2021

SCRIPTURE READING

1 JOHN 2:1–6

*But the love of God is truly perfected in whoever keeps
his word. This is how we know we are in him. The one
who claims to remain in him ought to live in the same
way as he [Jesus] lived.*

—1 JOHN 2:5-6

The hustle and bustle of this season can become overwhelming if we aren't careful. In our hurrying from
here to there, in our busyness with all the special activities and events, we tend to lose our focus. While we
try to honor the Christ child and celebrate the beauty
of the incarnation, we can rush right by the impor-
tance of this high and holy season.

Kosuke Koyama, a Japanese missionary to Thailand,
wrote about the speed at which God walks. Koyama
believed God came in a slow time, technologically, to
model for us God's willingness to be slow for us. Not
only did Jesus walk most everywhere he went, but he
also slowed to a complete stop for us on the cross. This
is an inefficient pace if you are trying to get things
done in our day and age. Koyama challenges us to
view love as a slow speed, and invites us to join.

The apostle John encourages the early church to obey
the words of Jesus. In obedience are joy and life! But
he also tells us that if we are obedient to God, and if

we remain in Jesus, we must walk as Jesus walked. This doesn't mean we try to find the most culturally accurate version of sandals that match what Jesus wore. It doesn't mean we need to go to the Middle East and attempt to trace Jesus's literal steps. It doesn't mean we can never get into a car, on a train, or board a plane because we need to walk everywhere. Although certainly these things could be meaningful and even enriching to our faith, that isn't the meaning of today's passage.

In this moment, what if we were to slow down? In this season, what if we were to be still? In this period, what if we took a deep breath, and then another?

When I am moving in a great flurry of activity and rushing from place to place I miss a lot. How can I see the people around me if I don't slow down? How can I see the love of God if I don't slow down? How can I demonstrate the deliberate love of Jesus to the world if I am always in a hurry? What does our rushing around show a world that hungers for the gift of the Christ child? What does our frantic activity communicate to those who need to know the King who will return?

What might happen if we slowed down, walking the speed of love, which may be slower than we like? How might this season of looking back and looking forward be different if we walk as Jesus walked? What new joy might we find?

FOR REFLECTION OR DISCUSSION

1. In what ways might you need to walk more like Jesus?

_____

_____

_____

_____

_____

_____

_____

_____

2. How does the idea of love being a slow speed impact your understanding of how we are to love God and love one another?

_____

_____

_____

_____

_____

_____

_____

_____

_____

_____

Friday, December 17, 2021

SCRIPTURE READING

PSALM 51

Have mercy on me, God, according to your faithful love! Wipe away my wrongdoings according to your great compassion! Wash me completely clean of my guilt; purify me from my sin!

Let me hear joy and celebration again; let the bones you crushed rejoice once more.

Please don't throw me out of your presence; please don't take your holy spirit away from me. Return the joy of your salvation to me and sustain me with a willing spirit. Then I will teach wrongdoers your ways, and sinners will come back to you.
—PSALM 51:1–2, 8, 11–13

Attributed to David after his abusive affair with Bathsheba and the murder of her husband, Uriah, Psalm 51 is a song of contrition, repentance, and guilt. David begs for mercy and forgiveness. David recognizes the truth of God's character. David realizes his sin. Knowing the horror of what he has done, he asks God to purify and cleanse and wash him. Knowing that his decisions have harmed his relationship with God and with people, he longs for the creation of something new in the place of the death and destruction he has caused.

In the midst of this psalm we find our word for the week, "joy." "Let me hear joy and celebration again," David prays. This implies that there is no rejoicing and no jubilation in David's life. And that is right. When we have given in to the temptation of sin, and then we come face to face with the wreck we have made of things, there should not be a party. Rather, in sober recognition of the damage we have done, with David we should cry out: "Have mercy on me!" or "Please don't throw me out of your presence." Sin is serious. There are consequences.

Yet one thing we can count on, even in our sin, is that God is merciful. We can be forgiven. As Paul reminds the people of the church in Rome, we don't go on sinning so that we can experience the forgiveness of God more and more. No! "All of us died to sin. How can we still live in it?" (Romans 6:2). When we confess our sin to the God who is merciful, we must also seek to follow the pattern of Christ. By grace we must die to sin as we continue to live for Christ. Transformed into the image of the one who came as a helpless baby and who will return as our reigning Lord and King, there is great joy in repentance and great joy in holiness. Like David, let's pray, "Return the joy of your salvation to me and sustain me with a willing spirit."

No matter where you are today on your faith journey, God is merciful. God is merciful to forgive those things you have done that you feel are unforgivable. God will restore you as you repent and seek to make right the brokenness your sin has caused. Don't wait! Receive the great gift of mercy. But once you have received it, do not fall back into a pattern of sin—rather, let God transform you!

What should we do? Today, let's bring the sacrifice of hearts that are humble and contrite and receive the deep and abiding joy that comes from the grace of God. Allow the Holy Spirit to fill you so you do not keep sinning but are given a willing spirit to live like Jesus.

FOR REFLECTION OR DISCUSSION

1. Is there someone in your life you have wronged? Write a prayer asking God to forgive you for what you have done.

_____

_____

_____

_____

_____

_____

_____

_____

_____

_____

_____

_____

_____

2. What are some practical steps you can take to ask the person you have hurt for forgiveness?

_____

_____

_____

_____

_____

_____

_____

_____

_____

_____

_____

_____

_____

_____

_____

_____

_____

_____

_____

_____

_____

_____

_____

The Lord Is Near

Saturday, December 18, 2021

SCRIPTURE READING

PHILIPPIANS 4:4-9

Be glad in the Lord always! Again I say, be glad! Let your gentleness show in your treatment of all people. The Lord is near. Don't be anxious about anything; rather, bring up all of your requests to God in your prayers and petitions, along with giving thanks. Then the peace of God that exceeds all understanding will keep your hearts and minds safe in Christ Jesus. From now on, brothers and sisters, if anything is excellent and if anything is admirable, focus your thoughts on these things: all that is true, all that is holy, all that is just, all that is pure, all that is lovely, and all that is worthy of praise. Practice these things: whatever you learned, received, heard, or saw in us. The God of peace will be with you.

—PHILIPPIANS 4:4-9

When I was in elementary school my dad, a pastor, would wait until I got home to go on hospital calls so he could take me with him. We would visit someone who was sick or who'd had surgery or given birth to a baby. It was such a special time to be with him. I can remember the numerous times my dad quoted this Philippians passage to hospital patients. But I've heard these words from my dad's lips at other times too—when I have been stressed about school or worried about something in a church I pastor. Probably by accident more than intention, I committed this passage to memory many years ago. I have heard these words frequently, and they are carved into my heart. I am grateful for how quickly they come to mind when I wrestle with the struggles of this life.

Our struggles are real, but God's grace is sufficient. These words of Paul remind us of who we are and who we are meant to be in this world. They also remind us of the God who is with us. This passage of Scripture is not a flippant response to trouble in the world. It is a reminder that, in the midst of that trouble, we can rejoice. Too often Christians want to sweep the problems around us under the rug with platitudes and easy answers: *Have more faith! Be happy! Don't cause disunity! It will get better!* Paul, writing to the church in Philippi, is having none of that. He is writing in response to the real problems we face.

Rejoice—because there is much to be sorrowful about. Be gentle—there are enough people who are rough, and rude, and harsh. Know that God is close—even though you might not feel like God is. Don't be anxious—even though there are plenty of things that cause anxiety. Embrace the peace of God in a world of turmoil. As Christians we aren't called to pretend all is well. We are called to follow a Savior who is with us no matter what we face. God's presence changes everything. How do we do this? We bring it all to God in prayer.

What would happen in our lives if we *really* brought all our needs, with thanksgiving, to God in prayer? How would we, our families, our communities, our churches, our workplaces, our nations, and our world be different if we followed the advice of Paul? Today is a good day to commit these words to memory, not just for the sake of knowing them but so they can be carved into our hearts. The Prince of Peace wants to guard our hearts in the midst of whatever we face. As we lean on him we will be able to rejoice no matter the circumstances. For this I am so grateful.

FOR REFLECTION OR DISCUSSION

1. List some things you are grateful for. Tell God thanks!

_____

_____

_____

_____

_____

_____

_____

2. What are some of the needs you have? List them here.

_____

_____

_____

_____

_____

_____

_____

3. One way to memorize something is to write it down. Use this space to copy down this passage of Scripture as you commit it to your memory.

_____

_____

_____

_____

_____

_____

_____

_____

_____

_____

_____

_____

_____

_____

_____

_____

_____

_____

_____

_____

_____

_____

FOURTH SUNDAY OF ADVENT

December 19, 2021

SCRIPTURE READING

LUKE 1:46–55

Mary said, "With all my heart I glorify the Lord! In the depths of who I am I rejoice in God my savior. He has looked with favor on the low status of his servant. Look! From now on, everyone will consider me highly favored because the mighty one has done great things for me. Holy is his name. He shows mercy to everyone, from one generation to the next, who honors him as God. He has shown strength with his arm. He has scattered those with arrogant thoughts and proud inclinations. He has pulled the powerful down from their thrones and lifted up the lowly. He has filled the hungry with good things and sent the rich away empty-handed. He has come to the aid of his servant Israel, remembering his mercy, just as he promised to our ancestors, to Abraham and to Abraham's descendants forever."
—LUKE 1:46–55

Mary's song recorded here in Luke 1 is beautiful. Through song, she reflects on and responds to her love for God and God's work in the world, and what her present experience will do through history. It is a beautiful song, but it's also subversive.

Zechariah, a priest in the Lord's temple, was given a promise of a child just like Mary. The angel came to him like the angel came to Mary. The child that was to be born to Mary was going to save everyone, and the child born to Zechariah and Elizabeth would play an important role in what Mary's child would do. Both women's bellies became round as their sons grew in their wombs; these two stories have much in common. The subversive part comes in the fact that Zechariah is silenced while a humble virgin teenager is allowed to sing. It upsets the normal systems for a powerful man in a religious position to doubt and question while Mary—who represents the epitome of weakness—accepts what God asks her to do.

Things are turned upside down. Mary tells us this very thing as she sings of how God will turn away the rich and satiated and lift the poor and the hungry. Mary offers a foretaste of what her Son will do when she raises her voice to sing of the arrogant who will be brought low. Mary sings the song of heaven when she declares how power is shaped in the kingdom of God.

Mary demonstrates for us that surprising people are called by God. People we don't expect can be deeply connected to God's will and way in the world. Zechariah doesn't surprise us, but an ordinary peasant girl? That should surprise us. And that surprise should lead us on a lifelong journey of looking for the places where God is at work that we would never expect. Who in our family, our church, or our community is singing, "With all my heart I glorify the Lord!"? Who in our schools, workplaces, or favorite restaurants is lifting their voices to say, "In the depths of who I am I rejoice in God my savior"? The truth of the matter is that God looked with favor on Mary, but we also believe God looks with favor on *all* people. So who is singing a song of praise? Who is pointing out the way the kingdom of God looks different from the kingdoms of this world? Who is reminding us of the faithfulness of God down through the generations?

What would happen if we began to look in new places for the way God is birthing the kingdom? How would I be different if the usual voices I listen to were silenced for a while and someone else was invited to speak? How would our churches be different if we began to seek the voice of God from the mouths of the unexpected, the socially marginalized, and the young? How might the gospel be spread if we listened more?

Love requires listening. Zechariah gets to sing later, but not right now. Right now, Mary sings. She sings of her great love for the God who does amazing things in unexpected ways. If we are to love God, we need to listen to one another. To love one another, we need to listen to God. The two work together. And when we listen, we may be surprised to hear the good work, the challenging work, the overthrowing work, the subversive work that God wants to do in us and through us.

Mary's response when the angel tells her what is about to happen is the response I want to have. Today, as I look back to the birth of her baby, Jesus, and look forward to the return of our risen Christ I want to say with Mary, "I am the Lord's servant. Let it be with me just as you have said" (Luke 1:38). As we learn from Mary to honor God with all we are and all we have, may we receive the call God has placed on our lives with powerful humility. As we participate with God, love will be born in us.

FOR REFLECTION OR DISCUSSION

1. Who are some surprising people you have learned from in your lifetime? Why was it surprising?

2. How might you respond to Mary's song today?

Monday, December 20, 2021

SCRIPTURE READING

RUTH

But Ruth replied, "Don't urge me to abandon you, to turn back from following after you. Wherever you go, I will go; and wherever you stay, I will stay. Your people will be my people, and your God will be my God. Wherever you die, I will die, and there I will be buried. May the LORD do this to me and more so if even death separates me from you."

—RUTH 1:16-17

The story of Ruth is another story of an unexpected person being pulled into the kingdom of God. The book of Judges ends with the troubling statement, "In those days there was no king in Israel; each person did what they thought to be right" (21:25). Some people chose good in those days, and others chose evil.

Ruth, the book that follows Judges in the Old Testament, begins with a family making a difficult choice. They left the promised land during a famine and went to Moab, where they thought they might have food. What happened to the family of Elimelech and Naomi was intensely destructive. They may have found food, but they also suffered great loss. Elimelech died, leaving their two sons to take care of Naomi. The sons got married, and then they too died. Left with no one to care for them in a land where you needed men to survive, Naomi started back to her homeland, to Bethlehem. She tried to prevent the widows of her two sons from going with her because their home was in Moab—they were not Israelite women, they were Moabite women. We do not fault Orpah, the one who chose to stay in Moab. But we pay close attention to Ruth, the one who refused to leave Naomi's side.

In Hebrew, the beautiful speech we read in English that Ruth gives to Naomi on the road is much more matter of fact than we realize. The poetic English says, "Wherever you go, I will go; and wherever you stay, I will stay." A direct, word-for-word translation from the Hebrew would sound more like, "You go, I go. You stay, I stay." Ruth is emphatic. There is a bond—there is love between these two in the midst of terrible tragedy.

Ruth's position as an outsider becomes more clear when they return to Bethlehem. Throughout this short book of the Bible, Ruth is rarely called by her name. Instead, she is most often recognized by her cultural and ethnic background as an outsider—a Moabite. It is clear that this designation is meant to make the hearers of this story pay attention. This *outsider* is the one who is doing the good and right things in the story. Making small, faithful choices—sometimes difficult choices but always kind choices—Ruth changes Naomi's life. They are no longer hungry because of what she did, and in the end she is able to bring Naomi great joy when she marries and gives birth to a baby to extend the family line.

The beauty and power of this story isn't just for Naomi and Ruth. This story has radically changed your life and mine—and the genealogy listed in Matthew 1 tells us why. Ruth—an outsider, a woman, someone who should not be connected to the people of God by all of the normal standards of the day—is listed as one of those from whom our Lord and Savior is descended. "Boaz was the father of Obed, whose mother was Ruth. . . . Jacob was the father of Joseph, the husband of Mary—of whom Jesus was born, who is called the Christ" (Matthew 1:5b, 16).

God used Ruth to carry on the family line that leads to the birth of Jesus. Why? Because with God there are no insiders or outsiders. All are invited to partner with God in the renewal of all things. Maybe you feel like an outsider. In the kingdom of God, there is no such thing! Hear the good news! You are invited. Or maybe you are a firm insider. In the kingdom of God, may we have such imagination that God uses unlikely people in the world. Hear the good news! God has made room for you and will make room for others too. Ruth is an ancient echo to Mary and can be an ancient echo for us. When God leads, may we respond with, "You go, I go." As we journey with God, we will be transformed by love.

FOR REFLECTION OR DISCUSSION

1. What is a challenging decision you made that didn't seem to make sense to those around you? Why did you make that decision?

    _____

    _____

    _____

    _____

    _____

2. How has the love someone had for you changed the trajectory of your life?

    _____

    _____

    _____

    _____

    _____

3. How can you embody love today?

    _____

    _____

    _____

    _____

    _____

SCRIPTURE READING

ROMANS 8:31–39

Who will separate us from Christ's love? Will we be separated by trouble, or distress, or harassment, or famine, or nakedness, or danger, or sword?

I'm convinced that nothing can separate us from God's love in Christ Jesus our Lord: not death or life, not angels or rulers, not present things or future things, not powers or height or depth, or any other thing that is created.
—ROMANS 8:35, 38–39

I have had the privilege of spending time at the Kakuma Refugee Camp in Kenya. Getting to see the way pastors—who have been forced from their home-land because of violence—minister to the people there changed my life. Taking their ministry with them, they illustrate for us in living color that "nothing can separate us from God's love in Christ Jesus our Lord." God's love is always there no matter what we face. In the midst of famine and violence, nothing can separate us. Phew! In the midst of hatred and discord, nothing can separate us. I'm so glad! In the midst of nakedness and distress, nothing can separate us. Perfect!

While it is true that God is for us and with us no matter what we face, we must be careful not to allow this truth to cause us to sit on our hands and do noth-ing. Right before our passage for today, Paul writes about how the goal for our lives is to be "conformed to the image of [God's] Son" (v. 29). What is the image of Christ we are being conformed to? In love, Christ came to free us from the oppression of sin and brokenness of this world. In love, Christ came to bring peace. In love, Christ came to heal people so they could be restored to the community. In love, Christ came to feed the hungry. As we are conformed to the image of Christ we too will grow in love. This love will lead us to action in the world.

Although the love of God has been and will continue to be with my friends in the Kakuma Refugee Camp, that isn't all there is. Conformed to the image of Christ in love, we *act* to bring peace and life and plenty. We work until there are no more refugees. The sweeping victory we win in Christ is like this time of year—it is present but not yet fully realized. In the Christ child, we see the great love of God for us. In the King who will return, we see the one who will establish the new heaven and the new earth. While we remember and while we wait we also work, in love, to show love to a broken world. For "I'm convinced that nothing can separate us from God's love in Christ Jesus our Lord."

FOR REFLECTION OR DISCUSSION

1. What are some ways you have experienced the love of God in your life?

_____

_____

_____

_____

_____

_____

_____

_____

_____

_____

2. How does knowing we can't be separated from God's love change the way you live?

_____

_____

_____

_____

_____

_____

_____

_____

_____

_____

SCRIPTURE READING

PHILIPPIANS 1:3-11

I thank my God every time I mention you in my prayers. I'm thankful for all of you every time I pray, and it's always a prayer full of joy.

This is my prayer: that your love might become even more and more rich with knowledge and all kinds of insight. I pray this so that you will be able to decide what really matters and so you will be sincere and blameless on the day of Christ. I pray that you will then be filled with the fruit of righteousness, which comes from Jesus Christ, in order to give glory and praise to God.
—PHILIPPIANS 1:3-4, 9-11

Paul, writing from prison, overflows with gratitude, which seems strange given his circumstances. Yet in writings we see again and again that it isn't where Paul is, or even what he is experiencing, that determines what he believes about God. God has saved his life. This mindset frames what he writes to the people of the church in Philippi. Paul reminds them that they are partners in the work of sharing the good news and changing the world around them. Paul honors them and their efforts to follow Jesus. Paul prays for them.

In 2020 many of us had a very bad year in which the word "unprecedented" was applicable to many events, especially in the United States: a global pandemic that took the lives of hundreds of thousands, unchecked forest fires, renewed civil rights protests and simmering racial tensions, yet another hostile and divisive presidential election, and that's just the big stuff. Life in the United States was not ideal for most of us in 2020, and division in the church only added fuel to the many metaphorical fires we fought all year. Paul's prayer is not being answered in the way we American Christians have responded to conflict and interacted with one another in recent months and years. Our love is not, as Paul hoped, becoming more and more rich.

God's love is infinitely rich. God's love is without measure. Nothing can separate us from the love of God in Christ Jesus. If this is so, why is our love for one another so easily forgotten when we disagree? Why is our love for one another sometimes shallow? As those who have received the agape, infinite love of God, why is our love so finite in response? Paul prayed that the people in Philippi would grow to love in this way "so that you will be able to decide what really matters and so you will be sincere and blameless on the day of Christ." We believe too often that we know what really matters. I have my very strong opinions about many things, and of course I believe it *really* matters. Laid at the feet of Jesus, though, I wonder how much it really does matter.

A rich love, a deepening love, a love that is discerning, is a God-like love. It isn't something I can drum up or create on my own. This kind of love comes from the grace of God at work in me. In the midst of my circumstances and yours, will we allow this grace, this lavish love of God, to change us? These lines we draw don't mirror the God who loves us. God's infinite love beckons all, makes space for all, reaches out to all. May Paul's prayer for the early Christians echo down into our hearts. What really matters? A baby in a manger who has come to change the world. What really matters? A coming King who will reign with justice, bring peace, and restore all things. While we look back and while we wait for the future, let's allow God's infinite love to help our love become more and more rich.

FOR REFLECTION OR DISCUSSION

1. What are some of the circumstances of life that make godly love difficult for you?

_____

_____

_____

_____

_____

_____

_____

_____

_____

_____

_____

_____

_____

2. How does God's infinite love change your perspective on the people and the world around you?

_____

_____

_____

_____

_____

_____

_____

_____

_____

_____

3. What is one opinion that you hold very dear? Does holding onto it tightly increase or decrease your love? Why?

_____

_____

_____

_____

_____

_____

_____

_____

_____

_____

Thursday, December 23, 2021

SCRIPTURE READING

MATTHEW 25:31-46

All the nations will be gathered in front of him. He will separate them from each other, just as a shepherd separates the sheep from the goats.

"I was hungry and you gave me food to eat. I was thirsty and you gave me a drink. I was a stranger and you welcomed me. I was naked and you gave me clothes to wear. I was sick and you took care of me. I was in prison and you visited me."

Then the king will reply to them, "I assure you that when you have done it for one of the least of these brothers and sisters of mine, you have done it for me."
—MATTHEW 25:32, 35-36, 40

Anytime we start talking about sheep, goats, and judgment people get nervous—and rightfully so! I don't know anyone who follows Jesus who doesn't sometimes wonder, *Am I with the sheep or the goats?* Jesus's teaching in our passage for today gives us some practical steps to take as we seek to live in loving relationship with God and neighbor. Although there are some specific actions mentioned in this text, it is important to pay attention not just to the literal doing of these particular things but also to the heart behind the doing. We don't make a list of feeding the hungry, giving a drink to the thirsty, welcoming the stranger, clothing the naked, caring for the sick, and visiting the prisoner—only to check it off and feel like we have done our part. It is so much deeper than that.

Jesus illustrates this depth when he speaks of those who do not inherit the kingdom. They respond by asking a question, "When did we see you that way, Lord?" The king replies to them, "When you have done it for one of the least of these brothers and sisters of mine, you have done it for me." In other words, when we see those who are marginalized, suffering, and oppressed not as strangers but as Jesus, then we know where we stand in the kingdom of God. The very fact that those who will be sent away in punishment want to know when they saw the king in those circumstances reveals something about their hearts. "If we had known it was you," they seem to say, "then we would have fed, clothed, welcomed, visited!" *If we had known it was you.*

Jesus invites us to recognize him any time we find a person in need. Serve, love, act as though it is Jesus in front of you. Mother Teresa, when asked about her love of God and people, talked about seeing Jesus in all his distressing disguises. We know our hearts are changed, and we know the love of God is at work in us when we can see Jesus in the hardest places, the most challenging people, and the most desolate realities. Our love compels us to see differently. Jesus is telling us to do it for them as if you knew it were me—*for it is me.*

We must remember that Christ the King is the one who separates the sheep from the goats. Too often we take on the role we have no business doing. We find ways to scapegoat those who are different than us, declaring who is in and who is out. Instead we need to recognize Jesus in all the people the world tells us are the other, loving radically like God loves us. I have found that engaging in acts of mercy like those listed in today's passage have deepened my love for the God who is merciful to me. I have also found that the more I love God, the more I can love my neighbors—all of my neighbors.

FOR REFLECTION OR DISCUSSION

1. What does God want to teach you from the scripture today?

_____

_____

_____

_____

_____

_____

2. What might you do in response to the scripture today?

_____

_____

_____

_____

_____

_____

Friday, December 24, 2021
CHRISTMAS EVE

SCRIPTURE READING

JOHN 3:16-17

God so loved the world that he gave his only Son, so that everyone who believes in him won't perish but will have eternal life. God didn't send his Son into the world to judge the world, but that the world might be saved through him.

—JOHN 3:16-17

Christmas Eve at my house always involves homemade bread and chili. We have a tradition of opening all of our gifts on Christmas Eve. My mom says the tradition started with her family and her dad's desire for the kids to know that Santa had nothing to do with the giving of gifts! Someone reads the birth narrative from the Gospel of Luke, and we pray together as a family, giving thanks for what God has done for us.

When I was little my dad pastored a church in Leavenworth, Washington. Leavenworth is a small town that re-styled itself as a Bavarian village when the logging industry died. During the winter, the town swelled with tourists from all around the world for the Christmas Lighting Festival. I remember the beauty of those lights flickering on after a countdown while we stood bundled in our coats and snow pants against the freezing cold. Our church was close to the downtown

that the World Might Be Saved

area and would do a living nativity every night of the week during the festival. People would walk over with their steaming cups of apple cider and stand on the snow-packed street. I loved being an angel in my polyester white robe that stretched over my snowsuit. My hands would be covered with white athletic socks while I waved my arms back and forth like wings. Occasionally a goat that was tethered nearby would get ahold of my costume, and I would have to fight it off. One of the best moments was when it came time for the baby to be born. Mary would go behind an evergreen tree, and someone would hand her a baby wrapped in a fur blanket. Sometimes, shocked by the cold air in its lungs, the baby would cry out.

"For God so loved the world . . ." What was God thinking? Verse 17 in this chapter of the Gospel of John is not as well known or loved as verse 16, but it helps us understand what God was thinking. God's desire is not to condemn but to save. This desire is wrapped up in God's great love for us. It is wrapped up in the skin and bones of a tiny baby whose cries echoed in the night. It is wrapped up in a long line of those who have gone before us, faithfully declaring that God is love. It is wrapped up in our hearts, our bodies, and our lives as we seek to live for Christ in the world.

I give my life to you, Lord.

I must decrease so Christ can increase.

What should we do?

I am the Lord's servant. May it be for me just as you have said.

Here I am, God, kneeling at the manger, longing for Christ's return.

Here I am, God, like a child waving her wings in a nativity scene, trying to be for the world a light in the darkness.

Here I am, God—it doesn't feel like I have much, but will you bless it and use it?

Here I am, God; I give my life to you.

Birth hope in and through me. Make peace in and through me. Bring joy in and through me. Pour out your love in and through me.

Come, peasant; come, king; and come, all in between, to honor the one who does not condemn but who is love. Receive the great gift of the King of kings and the Lord of lords.

FOR REFLECTION OR DISCUSSION

1. What are some of your family traditions that are important this time of year?

_____

_____

_____

_____

_____

_____

_____

_____

2. As you reflect on Jesus Christ, our Savior, as a helpless baby, how are you grateful for this gift?

_____

_____

_____

_____

_____

_____

_____

_____

_____

_____

3. The non-condemning love of God is such a gift! What is one way you can live in response to this gift?

_____

_____

_____

_____

_____

_____

_____

_____

_____

_____